The
Master
Musician

The Master Musician

Meditations on Jesus

*

JOHN MICHAEL TALBOT

ZondervanPublishingHouse
Grand Rapids, Michigan
A Division of HarperCollins*Publishers*

The Master Musician: Meditations on Jesus
Copyright © 1992 by John Michael Talbot

Requests for information should be addressed to:
Zondervan Publishing House, Grand Rapids, MI 49530

Library of Congress Cataloging-in-Publication Data
Talbot, John Michael.
    The master musician / by John Michael Talbot.
        p.   cm.
    ISBN 0-310-59790-0
    1. Providence and government of God. 2. Music—Religious aspects—Christianity. I. Title.
BT96.2.T35   1992
231'.5—dc20   92–17532
                                                                                CIP

This book is being released with the author's newest album, also called "The Master Musician," distributed by Sparrow and available in the music section of your local Christian bookstore.

Edited by Harold Fickett; Interior design by Bob Hudson

Printed in the United States of America

92 93 94 95 96 / BP / 10 9 8 7 6 5 4 3 2 1

This edition is printed on acid-free paper and meets the American National Standards Institute Z39.48 standard.

Contents

Introduction

*

*T*he Master Musician is a meditation on Jesus' work in our lives. To gain full benefit, it must be read in the same spirit in which it was written. It must be read as a meditation. It must be read as a sort of prayer. While it contains much teaching about life in Christ and the church, it is not a study. It is a meditation.

The work is divided into three main sections: God's grace, our human response, and life in the church. The first is likened unto the crafting of a fine guitar by the Master Musician. The second, unto our learning how to play under the Master's instruction. The third, unto learning how to play with others in the symphony orchestra or band.

It is my prayer that this little book will help to bring the readers into closer union with Jesus and into a more full communion, or "common union," with each other. Perhaps where page upon page of intellectual study has fallen short, this little simile in the parable tradition can open the doors of some of our hearts and minds more simply. After all, it is closer to the tradition in which Jesus Himself taught. Perhaps it will help bring us all closer to Him.

*The
Master
Musician*

I: God's Grace

*

God is the Master Musician. We are his instruments. He gently plucks the strings of our lives to make a harmonious song for all creation. We are like a beautifully crafted guitar, formed, seasoned, and brought to expression by the same hand.

The guitar is the gift of man. The tree and the forest are the gift of nature. All are gifts from God.

Before a guitar can be made, there must be a tree in the forest. The tree to be selected must be of just the right character. It must be straight and steady, not crooked and sickly. It must be at the right stage of growth because a tree too young does not yet possess enough of the strong wood. A tree too old has sections that are already hollow or even rotten. God knows just the right time.

It must be the right species. The oak, for instance, might make quality furniture and houses, but it makes a poor musical instrument. The tall pine, cedar, and spruce are much better suited.

Furthermore, some of the better wood can be found not in the tallest of trees but in those that are average and ordinary. Some that look stubby and short on the outside hold the best quality of wood within.

This is like God's choice of our own human life. God does not choose by appearance. Two people might both look tall, strong, and perfect at first glance, but God will choose one and leave the other at a given point in time. This is because God looks to the heart. He alone knows what lies within.

Furthermore, God will often choose the people whom the world considers weak to do his mighty work. They might look "short and stubby" by external appearance, but the "wood" of their hearts is just what God is looking for. They might well be short on the outside, but within they are destined to be mighty and tall.

Most of us are just "ordinary" trees. We are neither really tall or really short by the standards of the world. We just merge into the rest of the crowd. We are pretty much just like everyone else, but it is trees just as this that make up most of the world's greatest forests. God looks within and He is able to do His supernatural work in just the likes of us if we are willing to submit to the Master's hand.

But His hand will change us. We will never be the same. We will never be just a tree of the forest again. We must be made into something new.

*

The first change is the greatest: The tree must be chopped down. The once sturdy and tall tree must fall to the ground. Its strong and mighty branches that stretched out proudly in the clean mountain air must be brought down to the soil, clay, and rocks of the earth. This humiliation and death for the mighty and glorious tree are absolutely necessary before it can be transformed into a fine musical instrument, fit to play the music of God.

Likewise, our lives might be sturdy and strong in the natural state. They might be mighty and proud, but until they are cut down they cannot become a fine instrument for God. They must be crucified. They must be humbled. Then, and only then, can they be resurrected and glorified to make the mystical and supernatural music of Jesus. Only then can they be instruments of God.

The cut of the woodsman must be complete. It must cut across our whole way of life. It must cut at the very base of the tree, otherwise, the tree will not fall safely and correctly.

Therefore, the whole tree must fall. To get the best wood for the instrument, the trunk itself must be felled. It does not suffice to cut only a few branches.

The same holds true at the beginning of our life in Christ. The whole tree of our past way of life must be cut down. The cut must extend through every aspect of our past life. It must be at the base of all that we are in the world. If we try to save ourselves from this radical cut, the tree of our life will fall in a way that tears us to pieces, or opens us to disease and sickness. Neither the tree of our life will survive, nor will an instrument for God be made. The last state will be worse than the first. All will be lost. Only with a complete and clean cut at our life's base can the "best wood" of our life be found, reclaimed, and transformed into a beautiful instrument of God's music.

Many of us might be religious. We might attend church regularly, but until we let the cut of the Master sever every aspect of our life we cannot be made into something new, we cannot be born again. We are only beginners or perhaps have yet to really begin again.

Next, the craftsman must select the wood of just the right character and quality among the fallen trees. The wood must be of a certain age and quality to make a fine musical instrument and it must not be too green or newly cut. Furthermore, the grain must be consistent, tight, and narrow. Grain that is too wide often gives way to waves and even knots that threaten both the beauty and the strength of the instrument.

Some knots are permissible and even desirable. Some craftsmen and musicians think that knots add character to the instrument. Knots keep it from appearing artificial and sterile, more like a plastic computerized copy than the real thing. The same is true of our lives. Many of us still have "knots" in our lives. We are far from perfect. Perfection is not required—only the willingness to submit to the hand of the Master. He and He alone will craft us into a thing of beauty. He even uses the things that the world considers "flawed" to bring forth His perfection.

*

The wood is next cut into thin pieces. We might think it better to cut the wood into thicker pieces. Wouldn't the instrument be sturdier and stronger? Isn't it easier to cut a thick piece than a thin one?

The Master's logic says that the thinner the wood the better, for the thinner the wood is, the easier it vibrates in synchronization with the vibration of the plucked string.

Conversely, if the wood is too delicate and thin, it does bring weakness to the structure of the instrument. The wood must be thin enough to resound with the vibration of even the most delicate string but strong enough to withstand the bumps and hard knocks any musical instrument must eventually endure.

Likewise, for each of us it sometimes appears quicker, easier, and even safer to cut things in the thick and easy way. But the Master sees things differently. His way requires more time and skill. This is all necessary to make the music of God, which is both delicate and strong. By our own wisdom and skill such craftsmanship is impossible. We have only to submit to the skillful cut of the Master's hand.

*

After the wood has been carefully cut, it must be left to age again. Green wood can warp once the instrument is crafted. Furthermore, its sound is superficial and thin. The good craftsman looks for aged wood that will not warp once shaped into a fine instrument, and he looks for wood that will not only look good in shape but sound good in tone as well. After all, that is the primary reason for the guitar.

To accomplish this drying process, the wood is sometimes placed in a kiln. The heat cannot be too hot, or the wood will crack or burn, but it must be hot enough to dry the moisture from its deepest fiber. At other times the wood is left in dry storage for months and years at a time. This process is more natural, but it requires even more patience.

There is a drying process in our spiritual life as well. Sometimes external or artificial forces act on us in a way that seems almost too quick and intense. At times we think that we will surely crack or burn up in the intensity of this testing heat, but the Master will not allow the heat to get too hot. He has wonderful plans for the wood of our life once we have been dried out for a while.

Most of the time, the drying process is in the more natural and ordinary events and surroundings of daily life. Months and years drag on as we seem to just lie there with all the other drying wood. We go to school. We get an ordinary job. We get an ordinary job. We marry and raise ordinary kids. We seem stuck in the typical rut of modern living. Sometimes we think we have been totally forgotten.

But the Master has not forgotten. He knows the perfect time to begin the more active work. Something special is about to happen if we have the courage and the patience just to wait a little longer.

The pain in life is deep. For some its memory is still fresh and new . For others it is buried under years of continued denial. Hopes and dreams have also been forgotten over the years, hopes and dreams of the ideals and life found only in the real Jesus. We may have forgotten, but the Master has not forgotten.

His touch might bring pain, but it also brings healing. It transforms tears of sorrow and pain into tears of gratitude and joy.

*

Finally, the craftsman will select different kinds of wood for the different parts of the guitar. The body will be of one kind. The neck, of another. The fret board and bridge, of yet another. Furthermore, different wood will be selected for different sounds. Spruce is very deep and rich. Pine is very bright and clear. Cedar is balanced but not as sturdy. There are many different kinds of guitars; therefore, many different kinds of wood are needed. Each must be loved and appreciated for its unique gift.

There are also many different kinds of people, gifts, and talents needed in the body of Christ. Our gifts and talents are like the different woods of a superbly crafted instrument—in the end, they all work together, blend into the music God makes through us, adding unexpected resonances and colors that bring true and balanced richness to the overall sound.

*

Now the active work begins. The waiting is over. The selected wood must be cut and molded to fit the shape of the instrument. First, it is cut into proper shapes and sizes.

Some pieces must actually bend to form the proper curves in the shape of the guitar. This is done by adding moisture to the wood so that the wood will become pliable.

Without the moisture, the wood will simply break and crack. *We, too, must be shaped by God.* Some of this is done by further cutting. This means further crucifixion. It invariably means further pain, but it is necessary to get us into the right shape to be assembled by God.

We have already been cut down. We have already been through the extraordinary fire of the kiln. We have already endured the ordinary drying process of everyday life. We will, no doubt, object to further cutting, further pain, further crucifixion. Isn't it about time that the Master simply transforms us into His instrument?

But that is not the way it happens. Only those who are willing to go through this further pain will have the wood of their life cut into the appropriate sizes to craft the instrument of God. Otherwise everything up until now will simply have been wasted. It will have been in vain.

*

There are other areas, however, where further cutting simply will not do. We need to be gently but firmly bent and molded. This involves a lot of "stretching." But without being softened by the Holy Spirit, this can never be done. Without the Spirit's first "softening the wood," we will simply crack and break. This is a process of gentle care.

First, the Lord softens us with the moisture of the Spirit. Then He carefully and slowly bends us with a touch that is both gentle and firm.

Here the Lord takes the wood of our life and bends us in a direction we have never gone before. This is not the haphazard warpage of green wood. This is the intentional bending of our life into a whole new direction in conformity to the Master's plan. His hand is gentle, but it is also firm. The change must occur if we are to be a work of the Master. We must trust that He will give us the moisture of the Spirit. We must trust that He will not bend us too fast. The Master has no desire for us to splinter and crack at this point of our life.

Many of us remember the almost incomprehensible changes we have been through. Without the gift of the Spirit this, no doubt, would never have occurred. We have prayed. Others have prayed. God has responded. He has caused us to change our minda. He has helped us to change the whole direction of our lives. Truly some of us see that these changes have literally saved our lives. We have experienced the true meaning of salvation.

Others have resisted the Master's bending hand and simply remain as they were. Their unhappiness and sense of unfulfillment is left unchanged. They have yet to be saved.

*

The actual shape of the guitar is also important. Over the years, luthiers—or guitar makers—have discovered that a definite mathematical proportion in shape is important to ensure good tone. A haphazard layout of the shape creates real tonal problems. The wrong proportion here or there can create overtones that destroy the evenness or purity of the tone of each and every note that can possibly be played on the instrument. Some cold, hard, mathematical realities are very important to the playing of good music.

There are also hard, cold facts involved in the deeper mysteries of the music of God. Certain truths must be learned if our instrument is to be constructed correctly. Otherwise, our life might be filled with bothersome spiritual overtones that detract from the overall music of the Spirit. These truths do not seem very "musical" at first. They seem to be unrelated to our mystical life in God. But they must be learned and practiced before we can become an instrument of precise quality fit for the Master Musician.

Many of us want God, but we do not want to go through the "work" of the relationship of real love. We want it easy. We want it fast. But real work must be done before the perfection of a real love relationship with God can be experienced. We are also a perfect work of God in ourselves. What a work of God's perfection is the human being! The human body is far superior to even the most sophisticated of humankind's machines. Then there is all creation! Even the best scientists have yet to comprehend even minimally the universe or the world. Then there is the invisible realm of the spirit. If we cannot begin to understand that which is seen, how much less must we really comprehend that which is unseen. No doubt, the perfect work of God in humankind and all the universe of creation is a wonder to behold! God's Creation is a marvel.

The instrument is then assembled. Different pieces are glued together carefully. At first they are held in clamps. These clamps seem artificial and ugly, but they are necessary to ensure that the glued wood dries together properly. It is important that these clamps are strong and sure, but it is also important to ensure that the clamps do not mark or move the wood out of alignment. This is done by padding the brute force of the clamps with felt or cloth.

When our spiritual life is being assembled, we, too, must be glued and clamped. Remember that our natural state is only that of a wild tree in a forest. We are being made into something supernatural and new. We are being "re-formed." So, we must be artificially "forced" into the new form of a "guitar" before it becomes "natural" for us. We must be "clamped." We must be "glued." This means that we must be disciplined from without. Rarely do we have the strength from within to remain in this new position and shape until the glue fully dries.

This discipline usually comes from God through the church. It is important to have a pastor, spiritual director—or mature counselor and community to help mold you. But it is also important for the "clamps" to be cushioned. The discipline of truth without any cushion of tenderness, mercy, love, and care can leave a lasting scratch or more on the finish of the instrument. It can leave a permanent scar.

Once the instrument is initially assembled, you can begin to see the true shape of the guitar for the first time. This is an exciting moment. The assembled guitar tempts us to string it up and try to play a tune. But all is not complete. There is still much work to do before the guitar can make beautiful music.

It would also be easy to rush the process of our own spiritual development in Christ. Just because the basic shape of our new form is now apparent does not mean that we are ready to make music for God. There is still much work to do before we are ready to be what we have been created to be. Many Christians destroy God's greater work by rushing into a vocation or ministry at this point. Many deprive themselves and the world of the greater music of God by rushing the process.

Next, the wood must be sanded down to a smooth finish.

Here, all of the little imperfections and rough edges of the wood are sanded out.

Then a fine finish of lacquer is put over the sanded wood and allowed to dry fully.

This process is repeated many times, each time with a finer roughness of sander, until the finish is perfectly smooth.

This process is absolutely essential for the tone of the guitar as well as for the structural safety of the wood and the artistic beauty of the instrument. If one rushes this stage, all of the work up until now will have been for nothing. Impatience will have destroyed a potentially fine work.

Here we encounter the cross once more. Even though we think our new form, our instrument, is finished, it is not yet ready to make good music. There is still more pain to face. The sandpaper rubs out our obscure imperfections. Since the imperfections are increasingly obscure, the sanding process usually comes in ways we least expect. If often comes simply by living in community with our brothers and sisters. The rubbing of the sandpaper can be at first agitating and then become monotonous and tiring, but is absolutely necessary before applying the shiny gloss of the lacquer.

Have we really seen the day-in and day-out ups and downs of life with others in our towns, our churches, or our families as gifts from God? Or have we simply seen it all as a hassle and a pain? Perhaps if we saw it as God's "sanding process," we would be less disturbed and more loving with those with whom we live, work, and worship.

Many people think the lacquer is needed only for show . . . to make the instrument look beautiful. But this isn't true. Without the hard finish of lacquer, the instrument will neither sound right nor be structurally strong.

The lacquer process is long. First the wood is totally covered. Here we almost feel suffocated by the coating of God. We must wait patiently for this coating of God to dry. Then the lacquer is itself sanded and buffed before being lacquered over again. This happens as many as seven times before the guitar is ready. We, too, must repeatedly be sanded and lacquered over to be fine enough and strong enough to make beautiful music for God.

Yes we sometimes feel this "suffocation." We feel suffocated by the world. We feel suffocated in relationships. Sometimes we even feel suffocated in our church or Christian community. This suffocation is part of the death process in Christ. It is needed to help make our lives truly beautiful for God. We just wish most of the time that it didn't have to take so long.

*

Finally, the guitar is ready to string and play. Notice that in stringing the instrument, there is tension. Without reaching just the right tension, the strings will not resound on the right notes. Too little tension and there is a rattle or no sound at all. Too much and the string will break.

Tension is also a normal and healthy part of life in the church. If you are never "stretched," you will never play your true part. If you are stretched too much, you will surely break and be of no use to anyone. It is important to find the right balance in this tension so that we can sound the right note in the spiritual symphony.

Today we know about tension or stress. Some have simply had too much and have snapped. A list of those who have burned out or broken down comes to mind like a players' injury list before a big game. These are the overachievers.

Others run from tension of any kind and simply flounder like a loose guitar string, unable to make any real music with their lives. These are the underachievers.

Also, we cannot help but notice how little real beauty there is in the music of our modern world. Our radios, stereos, and music channels on television seem to play constantly. Music is everywhere—in the home, the car, the office, and the high-rise elevator. It is even in the church. Yet there seems so little real and lasting beauty in any of it . . . so little to uplift the soul. It has reflected the chaos and inhumanity of our culture well, but it has done little to change our culture for the better. The music of our modern world is little or nothing like the music of the Master. The perfect balance of creative tension is needed before the strings of our life can resound to make beautiful music.

*

This is not the end, however. It is the beginning. The guitar, when crafted with artistry and skill, must be played with equal love and care. At first even the finest new guitar will sound a little "green."

It will take a few years to mellow and mature. At this point even an older guitar of lesser craftsmanship and quality might still sound better to the average ear. Only those with a trained ear will hear the potential in this new instrument. At this point it should be played with regularity and love. A guitar's tone shapes itself to the style of the player.

Nevertheless, surprises have been known to happen. Sometimes a guitar left in a case for years because of its "green" and "immature" tone emerges from its case as a real jewel of majestic tone and truly mellow glory.

There are many lessons here. Even though we seem to have reached the end, we are really only at the beginning. Our preparation may have been a long process, but now the real work starts. Everything up until now has just been preparation. True ministry lies ahead. We are only now being ordained for God's work.

At the beginning, no matter how good the training may have been, you will still be perceived as "green" when compared to older members or ministers. Their training may not have been as good. You may have been prepared more completely. But still they will make better music. They have had time to age. There is no way around this reality. There are no shortcuts. At this point it would be easy to give up, but this is precisely the time to keep going. Only by consistently being played by the hand of God will you be imperceptibly molded to the music He Himself makes. But it takes time.

Even for those who put themselves "back in the case," a surprise awaits. No training is ever wasted. Sometimes after years away from the faith or out of community or ministry, an individual will return and discover how good the craftsmanship of his training really was. He will discover after years away that he, too, has matured and that his instrument now makes for God music rich and mellow in tone.

II: Our Response

*

Now I will tell you a mystery. I have often found that the tone of music is found not as much in the quality of the musical instrument as in the quality of the musician. Granted, a real master musician will benefit from playing a masterfully crafted instrument. Most master musicians have gone to great lengths to acquire a fine instrument to play. But a real artist can make beautiful music from even the cheapest instrument, while a bad musician will sound bad even when playing an instrument of priceless artistry and worth. It has been said that a master's tone is in the fingers, not in the instrument. And that kind of tone does not get to the fingers unless it first comes from the *heart*.

The Musician

God Himself is the Master Musician. We are only his instruments. We cannot make music without His touch. Without the Musician, the instrument's whole purpose is pointless, futile, and vain. Without God's touch, we are incomplete and unfulfilled. Furthermore, the more the instrument is played by the hand of God, the more we are actually conformed to His melody and style. We vibrate to His rhythm and resonate to His tone. We *actually mature* and *mold* according to His tone. We are *conformed* to His image.

*

But here is the deeper mystery: We are also created in God's image. We, too, are musicians. Here we make the jump from being mere instruments to becoming co-creators as musicians and composers and from mere unregenerate humanity to the supernatural. We are co-heirs with Christ. We are "like Christ" as Christians. We are also called to be musicians with Him who is the first and last Master Musician.

True musicians must deeply love music. They must hear the inspiration of eternity behind the note, or the playing of the note will bring no lasting inspiration at all. They must hear the "universal language" that music is and desire to speak this language well. They must have broken through to the eternal through the hearing of a symphony or a song and truly desire to bring eternity to others. Otherwise their music remains only a technique, not true and lasting art.

As "musicians" of God, we must do far more than merely play "notes." Our study of Scripture or sacred tradition, or of creation itself, must be far more than mere theology. It must begin and end with prayer. It must be graced by the Spirit, or it will ever remain only a pursuit of the law. The law brings death. Only the Spirit brings beauty and life.

*

But this tone of the eternal also gets into the fingers through long and tedious work. Art must not only be inspired, it must be crafted and worked for to be achieved. If one is to develop the hands of an artist, the person must practice and play until his muscles ache and cramp and his fingers blister, cut, and bleed.

Many a concert have I played early in my musical vocation while nursing a finger cut deeply by the razor-like string of a steel-string folk guitar, and a fingernail pulled back to the quick by aggressively bending a string once too often. Similarly, in folk and classical playing I have learned to strengthen and guard the nails on my right hand after tearing them off through carelessness or abuse. Even playing properly, I've had to endure blisters, cuts, and bleeding fingers in order for layer after layer of calluses to develop. These have made my fingers look normal and even delicate again.

Enduring the aches and cramps builds up real strength. Then the hand is free to play hard or softly, quietly or loudly, tenderly or toughly. But underneath the delicate-looking hands of the guitarist are the strength of a carpenter and the calluses of a sailor. Delicate beauty does not come easily.

This means that the student and lover of God must lovingly study the long and varied experiences of God through God's many and various people, the church. We are only one small part of the church. If we truly want to know and love the universal fullness of the working of the Spirit of God, we must lovingly study how that same Spirit has worked in others around the world throughout history. If we have even the smallest measure of humility, we come to understand this reality, this need. Anything short of this is either shameless pride and arrogance, or the intentional deprivation of God from our soul. This, too, constitutes the ultimate pride.

This study does not mean that all are called to be scholars, for God knows that this, too, is often a road to pride. It simply means that we will avail ourselves of as much of the instruction of others as we can. It is an admission of our poverty. It is a work of humility. So, like the musician, we, too, must study and practice the rudiments and disciplines of our spiritual music or else our music will never be what God desires it to be.

Good music expresses the heart, but if you are to have the freedom to express the fullness of the heart, you must embrace the mundane discipline of repetition and practice. You must become a slave to the notes of the scale to make music. Only after you have become a slave to hour after hour of scales and lessons, will those scales and lessons become your servant so that you can freely express the music of your heart. But you must concentrate and force all your attention on mundane notes and scales before you can play notes and scales in the midst of inspiration and song without worrying about them at all.

This means that we must be willing to study how God has worked in traditions other than our own. The charismatic must learn of the contemplative—and the contemplative, the charismatic. The liturgical and sacramental must learn the freedom of the spontaneous, and the spontaneous must learn the beauty of the liturgical and sacramental. The low church must stretch to the high, and the high must be humbled below the low. The Catholic must learn of her own gifts from the Protestants who have often used her own gifts better than she herself has, and Protestants must learn to see the universal richness of the Catholics, which they may not yet possess fully themselves. This all involves much humility and much patient effort. But it always results in much growth.

Only after growing acquainted with others' approaches to

God will you discover what is truly yours. You will discover your own unique combination of the truths of all these legitimate ways to God. You will no longer be intimidated by this richness. You will be enriched by it.

Sometimes your lesson will make you play a style that you are not comfortable with. It will cause you to stretch. This is not the passive stretching of the wood under the hands of the Master. This is responsive. This is our active response to the lesson of the Master Musician to learn to play a musical style or technique that we would not normally even be attracted to. It is an active response of obedience. But you must learn it anyway. It is only after mastering a great many styles and techniques of others that you will really discover your own.

The scales or chordal position may stretch your fingers in a way they are not accustomed to. Only after they are comfortable with these new positions are you really free to choose to use them or not, or to use them in your own way. Until you master them, you are not really free to choose. You are still mastered by them.

Form and Power

When learning to play the guitar, begin with holding the instrument properly. Before you can learn to play the instrument, you must first learn proper posture. You must learn how to sit, how to hold the guitar, where and how to pluck and finger the strings, where to hold your arm and hand to properly finger the fret board. Ironically, if you do not first learn how to do all of these seemingly insignificant things, you will later find yourself hindered from playing the more artistically challenging pieces. If you do not learn how to pluck the strings properly from the proper hand position, your tone will be forever inferior.

It is also important to learn the forms of the faith. Christianity has certain doctrines, sacraments, and church structures. Classical Christian spirituality, as well, has certain disciplines that wise elders teach novices. These are important. Unless we take the time to learn these forms, we may later find ourselves hindered in the deeper things of the Spirit.

But if all we do is learn the "form" of playing the guitar without ever really making good music, we then have only the "appearance" of a good musician.

In the same way, if all we do is learn forms of religion without going on into the power of religion, then we have only accomplished a religion that is pointless and vain. Just as the well-positioned guitarist must go on to make good music if his form is going to accomplish its goal, so must the follower of Christ go on to discover the power of the Spirit.

Singing

Singing is a similar discipline. Perhaps the most pure instrument of all is the human voice. Some people say that they cannot sing at all. This is usually untrue. Most people can sing if they really want to. It just takes determination and practice.

I began to sing simply by singing. At first I didn't sound very good at all. It would have been easy for me and others to say that singing was not "my gift" at this point. But I kept singing. I could hold a note but without maintaining an even vibrato or rich tone. I just had an immature voice that could sing notes.

After years and years of singing, something happened. Seemingly out of nowhere a vibrato emerged. This made the notes more pleasurable both to sing and to hear. This gave me confidence. Then after many more years, my voice began to deepen and mellow. Almost without my knowing it, my voice could now express my heart.

The same thing is true of our study of God. At first it seems tedious and boring. Then we begin finding some joy in it, but we are still pretty much mimicking the lives and experiences of others, either living or dead. Then something mystical happens. Almost out of nowhere and overnight, in Christ and His church we find an identity and spirituality that is uniquely our own. It is our own special gift from Jesus. Suddenly we can "sing." Our voices become our own. We no longer "sound like" this or that person. We have become who we really are in Christ. After much study and labor, we have realized Jesus' gift of love to us.

Furthermore, this "voice" can really express the heart. No longer must we stumble across the endless references to others. Those references have become so second nature that we have simply absorbed them into our deepest soul in prayer, even as they once so absorbed us in study. Now we refer to them without trying. They are behind every word and every sentence we use. They simply *are*. Now instead of serving them with our mind, they serve our heart. They have become one with that heart in the Spirit.

Songwriting

A similar process holds true for songwriting. I began songwriting by simply writing songs. My older brother inspired me by writing his own. Somewhere deep inside of me I knew I had something to say. I didn't really yet know what, but I knew it was there inside just waiting to be discovered. So I began to work, to discover. I began writing songs.

At first, I toyed with using other peoples' lyrics. Composing was more my natural gift. Then I began writing lyrics as well.

For one solid year I wrote at least a song a day. I can remember my older brother's standing over my shoulder, tearing my songs and lyrics to pieces. "Why this phrase here? Why this melody there?"

I was devastated. These songs were "mine." How dare someone else tell me what is of worth when it comes from my heart?

This criticism hurt, but it was offered out of love and was absolutely necessary in developing my songwriting skill. Today I am sure the songs weren't really very good. I didn't keep even one of them. I don't even remember them today. But I remember the training. The training was priceless. It wouldn't have done its work, though, if my older brother and I hadn't had the courage and fortitude to learn to write songs by actually writing songs and submitting them to the scrutiny of others.

The same holds true of spiritual life in the church. We, too, must submit our journey in Christ to the scrutiny of another person or persons more experienced than ourselves. Like St. Paul, Christ's revelation must come personally and perhaps even directly to us without any human intermediary. But also like Paul, we must submit this revelation to the scrutiny of others to discern its validity and counsel. Many have been deceived and deluded by trying to follow the way of Christ alone.

This means submitting our own personal faith experience

and discernment of God's will to the help given us by God through the church. This comes through the ordained clerical leadership of the bishops and local pastors. It also comes through the clerical and lay leadership of the various communities, cell and support groups of the church. With these in place, it comes even more importantly through the input of a spiritual director or elder who very personally helps us to follow the way of Christ. This person may or may not be in any formal leadership position. But if he is truly an "elder" in the full sense of the word, his charismatic leadership will prove invaluable.

But one must follow the other. The discernment by legitimate church leadership always takes priority over the discernment of an isolated individual who claims the position of elder. As with St. Paul, this position is confirmed by the church if it is authentic. This keeps us from falling into cultic patterns of leadership or community. Like St. Paul, it keeps us from running in vain.

The art of songwriting has proven invaluable even in putting Scripture to music. To write a Scripture song, one has to know how to write a complete song on one's own. To use another's lyrics, you must learn the art of lyricism yourself. You must know where to change and adapt someone else's lyrics and why you are doing it. Sometimes you make changes to fit the music and meter. Sometimes to better harmonize the lyric and the music; sometimes to better relate the emotion of the lyric and music through the use of different vowel sounds. Using scriptural lyrics is a very subjective process but begins with a very real grasp of the objective facts.

Likewise, it is important to grasp certain disciplines of Scripture development and interpretation before trying to interpret Scripture extensively in your personal life. Many a false prophet has gone out into the world through such private interpretations. Without first humbly submitting to the disciplines of Scripture, we end up doing a disservice to Scripture by using Scripture improperly. Without a humble approach to these disciplines, we are reduced to the approach of pride.

Many have been cut to pieces by an insensitive use of Scripture. Many an interpretive argument has accelerated and smashed friendships, families, and even churches. The sword of God's word has not always been used to heal. It has been used to cut and maim. It has been used to kill.

What about the use of Scripture by those who founded our respective churches and denominations? No doubt we must all admit that many of the divisions in Christendom were caused by actions and reactions of both new founders and older church authorities who were reacting rather than responding with their use of Scripture. Reaction divides. Response heals and unites. So much pain and division could have been avoided if only we had submitted to the way of the Master; then our life could have become a living song.

Words and Music

To have a complete song, one must have words and music. Words without music are lifeless and cold. Music without words often lacks direction and clarity. By themselves, both words and music can be good. Words can be poems or short stories. Music can become a symphony. But it takes both words and music to make a song.

The same thing is true with Scripture and prayer. Scripture by itself is good but incomplete. When Scripture and prayer come together, they make a song. Likewise, the law of God is good, but without the Spirit it brings only condemnation, guilt, and death. The Spirit is good, but without the law the Spirit can be incorrectly discerned. We need both the law and the Spirit, the Scripture and prayer, to make the song of God.

The song is Jesus. He is the Word made flesh. He is the culmination of all human prayer. In Him, Scripture and prayer, the law and the Spirit, have come together to form the perfect and eternal song of humankind and of God.

Word Memorization

The words of songs, like the music, are best memorized if the performance is to be truly spontaneous and free. As long as the performer must constantly look down to the sheet music to read the words or music, he or she will always be somewhat intimidated. The performer will never really be free to let the song soar as an expression of his heart. When the song is really memorized, the musician is free to really make the song his own in performance. Only then can it also express the heart and soul of the listener.

It is the same with Scripture. Scripture is best memorized if it is to become second nature to all our thoughts. This is why the early monks spent their novitiate, or first years with the community, memorizing the entire Psalter and most of the New Testament. Memorization is equally good for the serious Christian today. The words of Scripture must become second nature to us and so sink deep into the heart. Then the words of Scripture will truly express our hearts and come to touch the hearts of others.

Musical Styles: Classical and Folk

Some students of classical music turn up their noses at popular or folk music. They consider it inferior. But almost all classical music was once folk music, adaptations of folk music, or at least the popular music of the upper class. The classical composers were often the ones "breaking all the rules" of traditional music. They were the elite pop musicians of their day. The "classicists" of their own day often considered them irreverent and vulgar. Now the irreverent are reverenced, and the vulgar considered cultured. The way they broke the rules has now been turned into a rule not to be broken. Perhaps we classical music lovers have missed the point.

Today's students of classical music rarely compose. Usually they can only study the work of composers. They have become so bound by their study of the past composers that they have discovered none of those composers' freedom to work for themselves. They can play notes off a page with precision but cannot improvise or compose them out of thin air.

The same holds true in spiritual things. We, too, have our "classical" and "folk" approaches. The "folk" musician of the Spirit is the simple saint of God who discovers the height of mystical prayer and sanctity by personal experience. The "classical musician" is the theologian or ecclesiastic who has made a science of studying the achievements of others yet achieves very little himself. In the end, they not only keep themselves from sainthood but try to prohibit the saint as well by looking down their sometimes long, snobbish noses of "classical music" at the poor "folk musician" of the Spirit, the real saint of God. In the end it is the "folk musician" of the Spirit who experiences the blessings of mystical prayer and sainthood in God. The "classical musician" is left forever on the outside looking in.

Music and Musicology

A brilliant theologian who is also a fine musician was once attending a symposium on Patristics (or the study of the writings of the church fathers). Talk after talk was given. Each talk was artistically crafted and profound in its observation of the spirituality of the early church fathers. Suddenly it dawned on my theologian/musician friend: This was wonderful "musicology" but not "music." It was all *about* spirituality, but it was not spirituality. It was all from the outside looking in.

God wants us on the inside. He does not want us to remain only musicologists. He wants us to make music.

Let us proceed to look at various styles and developments of musical history. But let us pray that we do not simply make observations about these musical styles and their relation to Christian spirituality. Let us pray that they help usher us into real spiritual union and development in Jesus Christ.

Primitive and Ancient Music

Music as we know it in the West is a fairly modern invention. But most of the music of human history, secular, or sacred, is ancient and primitive indeed. And it is often far more tonally expanded and exciting than our modern inventions. Ancient and primitive music is filled with pulsating rhythms, modal tones, and harmonies that seem strange to the modern ear, yet seem somehow familiar as they reach deep into the hidden, collective consciousness of our soul. Be it the early chants of the Christian church, or the early instrumental music of almost any culture of the world, there is a common thread of rhythm, modality, and tone that reaches deep into the human heart. Only much later does the music of Western civilization almost artificially limit and organize rhythm, modality, and tone into categories such as "major" and "minor" keys and harmonies, or the more boring and predictable rhythms of pop music.

To make the music of our universal and timeless God, we, too, must break out of our modern conception that dates back only a few hundred years. In expressions of worship and prayer, we must discover that song of the Spirit that cuts across all cultures, times, and peoples. We must discover the song of the Spirit that is truly universal and full, or "catholic." This will take us back to the origins, back to the beginning. Then and only then will we really be able to go confidently into the future.

Byzantine and Gregorian
Up to and into the Middle Ages (500–1430)

The earliest sacred music of the church existed alongside of and even preceded the primitive music of the Middle East and West. Though usually without instrumental accompaniment, this music is far from primitive. Its theology, ideology, and sound are rich and developed. Much like the seemingly more primitive yet richly symbolic and theologically developed painted icons of the same period in graphic art, so is the music of this period as contrasted to the later developments of the modern world.

The melodies of the musical art of the East may sound strange and unfamiliar to the modern Western ear, but its modes and scales are just as (and even far more) intricate and complex as anything developed in later periods. Likewise, the modes and scales of the Western Gregorian chant are paradoxically both more delicate and intricately human and simple than anything achieved in later periods. The "development" of later periods, while not bad in itself, often represents a loss rather than a gain in musical sensitivity. To ignore either of these sacred music expressions as "primitive" or "undeveloped" would be a tragic mistake. To throw them out would be a crime both to musical art and to God. It is encouraging to see many modern musicians rediscovering these ancient forms and integrating them into modern styles.

The same thing is true in church history. The earlier patristic period of the church represents a richly developed theology and spirituality unto itself. It comes before the later developments of the West, but it is not at all primitive. If anything, those who strictly adhere to this patristic spirituality, theology, and ecclesiology often consider the later expressions to be more of a degeneration than a true development. While I do not totally agree with this assessment, I do believe that there is some truth in it.

We, too, must really value the early pristine and pure patristic era of the faith if we are to safely adventure into the developments of the modern periods of church history and spirituality. Though we would not do well simply to discount all later developments, we would all do well to rediscover this wellspring of patristic wisdom before we too quickly consider our own modern philosophies, theologies, and spiritualities all that wise. Before we build on the foundations of the past, it is good to know what we are really building upon.

Renaissance (1430–1600), Baroque (late (1500–1790) and Classical (early 18th- to early 19th century)

Only slowly did the music of the West raise itself out of the mystical intuitions of the soul to the more calculated and precise intelligence of the mind. This happened in the development of what we now, at least popularly, call "classical music." You can see this as music developed from Gregorian chant to the polyphony of Palestrina, the instrumentally accompanied masses of William Byrd, and on to the orchestral and choral work of Bach, Handel, Vivaldi, Mozart, and early Beethoven.

Something was gained, yet something was lost.

On the positive side, this music ingeniously combines rhythms and harmonies both mathematically sophisticated and awe-inspiring in their simplicity. The true masterpieces developed expanded harmonics and tone through profound and simple melodies that still reached deep into the human heart. These harmonies built on and expanded the logic of the mind. They brought together logical truth and mystical love.

Of course, the ever-present danger in learning to appreciate and play this type of music is that in developing the genius of the mind, we forget the mystery of the heart. Many a 'classicist' has degenerated into a coldhearted technician. The heart must be retained, or the music of the soul becomes an expression of the living dead. It becomes vain.

We, too, must learn the "classics" of spirituality. Oh yes, they expand the logic of the mind precisely and with great ingenuity. But the true "masterpieces" always retain the ability to reach deep into the human heart where this logic acquires will and substance. True theology builds on the simple in order to discover the wise. Only this wisdom is divine. Only this spiritual music is "classical."

Romantic (1803–1900) early 19th- to early 20th century

Out of the mathematical development and precision of the Renaissance, the Baroque, and the Classical came the Romantic, as the yearnings of the human heart cried out to be recognized once more, along with and above mental speculation. This music uses all that had come before in the development of the mind to state the heart's sentiment. You can see this with later Beethoven, Borodin, Tchaikovsky, Bruckner, and even Mahler and Wagner. These composers varied in ethnic origin but are all considered Romantic greats.

Despite the many successes and beauties of the Romantic Period, it never really rediscovered the more primitive cries of the heart. It never penetrated to the more hidden depths of the soul. At times, its melodies were almost melodramatic. But at least the cries of the forgotten and silenced heart were being heard. The heart was being rediscovered.

The same thing happened in spirituality. As the scholastic theologians continued "organizing" the mysteries of God, the devotional life of the church at times became overly "romantic" in response. This gave rise to overly sweet and melodramatic concepts of the Sacred Heart of Jesus and the Passion of Christ. You can see this devotional pattern among Protestants and

Catholics alike. These subjects were good in themselves, and if used properly, can still be quite beneficial. But an artificial sentimentality kept them superficial, at least, and made them unbelievable to many.

On the positive side, the many Romantic devotions of the church gave expression to the mystical heart of the faith, God's love, especially through emphasizing the incarnational aspects of Jesus' life on earth. This was, after all, the greatest expression of God's love for humankind and all creation. In response to this wonderful mystery of love, can we ever really be "too romantic"?

Impressionism and Dissonance (1890–1920)
(late 19th- to early 20th century)

There is a form of musical art that grew out of and alongside of Romanticism called Impressionism. Impressionism tries to capture the non-geometric realities of nature in music.

This form of expression can be heard in the music of Debussy, Ravel, the tone poems of Respighi, and the beautiful Requiem of Fauré. Nature does not consist of perfect squares, rectangles, or circles, as implied in the Renaissance, Baroque, Classical and Romantic periods. It is made up of many irregular angles and shapes. There is no uniformity, yet a perfect unity remains. Perfect order and harmony remain even in the midst of apparent irregularity.

Mountains, hills, plains, and valleys; lakes and seas; trees, grass, and flowers; all of them make up a beautiful and unquestionable harmony. Yet none consists in geometric squares and right angles. Only humankind thinks of such things as perfect. Yet only we have been able to upset the balance of nature by the imposition of our superficial concept of "harmony" upon all creation. Impressionism tries to return to this deeper harmony musically.

Likewise, impressionism tries to capture things like the

non-resolution of a phenomenon in nature such as the ripples flowing out from a stone thrown into a pond, or body of water. Although these circles form a perfect symmetry, they never resolve back to the center. They always continue outward.

Musically these things are often expressed through the use of harmonic dissonance. Dissonance uses two or more clashing notes in the midst of an otherwise harmonious chord. These notes can be played together, or in a scale-like succession.

While the dissonance is displeasing and upsetting in itself, if played sensitively, it can actually sound peaceful and restful. It can help bring the listener into close union with God through these irregular aspects of nature. In like manner, this modern form hearkens back to the modal harmonies of ancient music in a developed and new way. It is old and rooted yet fresh and new.

The same thing is true in our spiritual life. Many times things seem to clash when looked upon only in themselves. In obedience to God, the church, and our community, things will not seem to make immediate sense. They may even seem to clash. But when we back off of the immediate "dissonance" of the events, we will discover a larger harmony in our lives that is "impressionistic." When we completely trust God, He will make of our lives an impressionistic music that brings harmony and peace even out of the seeming "dissonance" of obedience to God in all things.

For example, I have seen this in many marriages. Sometimes it seems irregular by today's cultural standards to stay with a spouse we have grown away from, or the spouse from us. The culture of today says that if it is becoming too uncomfortable, bail out of the marriage and find a new partner. For those who are obedient to the teachings of Christ and the church, we may find some very real non-resolution at first. But if we hang in there by faith, we will discover a deeper harmony through the dissonance. We will find a peace that passes all understanding that can save a marriage. It may take years. It may even take a lifetime. But the harmony and the peace will come for those who wait with the heart of faith, hope, and love.

It also works the other way around. What about when one's spouse leaves despite the other one's wishes? Frustration and despair are often the result of hanging on to a leaving spouse too long, or projecting one's own values upon him or her. There is a time to hang on. There is also a time, through prayer, to let go and release the person to God. God's "impressions" may bring about a greater harmony than is immediately apparent. It may sound like "dissonance" to us, but in the eternal music of God it may work a greater harmony of providence.

Similarly, when we first try to break free of the artificially geometric harmonies of the modern world, we might find the harmonies of God quite unfamiliar. We might even say that they clash. But if we play them in obedience to our Teacher by faith, soon we will discover a new and more expansive "harmony" than we ever knew before. Ironically, it will be rooted and ancient while still developing into something wonderfully fresh and new.

In the negative, it has been said that Impressionism reflects an "escape from reason" in the philosophical world that had such devastating effects on theology, affecting the faith and morality of the church. Here logic retreats from universal and timeless truths and knows only relative truths, which cause our whole world to reel and sway like a drunken sailor or a prizefighter about to fall after the final blow. No doubt, there is some truth to this observation.

But true impressionism works well when it builds on the truths of all that has come before. It is not meant to destroy. It is meant to build. It does not deny the concept of truth and stability. It expands it. It takes us beyond the limited perceptions of humankind to the expansive vision of God.

We frequently feel compelled to fall back into the same old comfortable lifestyle patterns and ruts of the secular and affluent

West when the teaching of God through community or the church seems to challenge or "clash" with our own will. This is true especially in the areas of morality such as Gospel simplicity in the face of Western materialism, gospel chastity in the face of Western promiscuity, and Gospel obedience in the face of Western individualism. It is hard to be conformed to the will of God, especially when we don't really understand it. It seems to call us higher. Sometimes it seems foolish to climb so high. Furthermore, there is the radical breakdown of values in our world. What is right? What is wrong? Nobody seems to know anymore. Some don't even care. The Scriptures and the teaching of the church provide some developed and balanced norms in the midst of our morally chaotic world. They provide stability and peace. Deeper peace awaits those who will let God's "impressions" flow into their soul. God knows that there are many who desperately need that peace.

Minimalism

Minimalism is even more modern and contemporary than impressionism. It is current in musical history and is represented by the religious and secular work of Steve Reich and John Adams. It creates the impression of waves of fluid tones and melodies by the rapid repetition and loops of single notes. Like impressionism, it seeks to create a sound much more broad than the particular notes played. If you focus on the notes, you find yourself getting agitated and nervous. If you just let go and "intuit" the whole of the sound, you find yourself almost floating in slow and fluid waves of total harmony and peace.

Unlike Impressionism, these particular notes and loops are very angular and mathematically precise in their nature, used to create an overall feeling or impression of wavelike fluidity. Ironically, this rapid-fire use of angular tone and notes creates the effect of "minimal" movement in slow waves of overall sound. If listened to without the wrong expectations, it sounds peaceful indeed.

The same thing holds true in our life with Christ. Sometimes things begin to move so fast that if we only focus on the immediate things to be done, we grow frantic and agitated. They seem angular, cold, and mathematically calculated in and of themselves. If we back off and intuit the whole "sound" of our lives, however, we will discover the fluidity of wave-like changes that bring life-giving peace and joy.

Many of the particular events and changes of our daily life may appear angular and overly calculated and mathematical. The mundane realities of daily lives often come in such rapid-fire succession that we fail to see the greater ebb and flow of life. Bills, jobs, and the particular events of raising a family, or leading a community, can often rob us of the deeper riches of living that pass over and through these seemingly relentless realities. But if we look to the whole picture, we can see that by faithfulness in these constant repetitions of angularly mundane and seemingly insignificant "notes" in our lives, a truly pleasing fluid-like wave of harmony and tone come from our lives.

God knows that the simple people of our world are also greatly affected and disturbed by the relentless and coglike unfolding of the mathematical machine of modern events. The modern world is hectic and fast paced. Politics and economics seem out of control. Shifts in global power are exciting. But they are also frightening. Wars and economic collapse are frequently in the air. How desperately we need to see the hand of God in the rapid-fire unfolding of these events. How desperately we need to break through to that peace in the midst of the storm . . . that peace that passes all understanding.

The Master knows our fear. He knows our weariness. He understands all too well. He takes us on to a music that helps bring us into a much needed rest.

Meditational Music: One Note, Many Notes

Sometimes in meditational, or what some call New Age music, one note stands out alone. This note communicates much more than just one note, however. The note is played with the authority of having played many notes. It comes from the authority of experience.

To play only one note effectively, the musician must be able to play many notes. He or she must be able to play the scales of virtuosity. Then he plays the simplicity of one note by choice and not just by the lack of skill. There is a world of practice and experience in the solitary sound of just one note. The note becomes authoritative. The note becomes mystical.

The same thing holds true with speech and silence in the wisdom of God. We need not buy into the theology of the 'New Age' to discover this priceless jewel of traditional Christianity. If you are able to say much, then you can say little with authority.

If you say much while being unable to say little, you come off as a talkative fool. If you say little because you are unable to say much, you remain a fool in the clutches of ignorance. If you say little with the authority of much knowledge, you discover real communication and the way of the wise. This is an age-old truth of the Christian faith, and can be found in the words of the sages of almost all religions.

The Space Between the Notes

Likewise, with meditational music: It is just as important to hear the space between the notes as it is to hear the notes played. Sometimes it is this space between the notes that actually makes the notes sound bigger. Consequently, the "bigger" sound is actually accomplished by playing less. Sometimes the silence and space communicate just as much as the sound.

So it is in Christ. Sometimes our silence says just as much, if not more, as our words. Sometimes silence is needed in order for words to really communicate.

Moderate Discipline

Within any of these musical forms, a musician can desire to practice diligently and become a true artist, only to get sidetracked and frustrated along the way. First, you can develop individual techniques that are contrary to the instruction of the teacher. No matter how small, these individual idiosyncrasies can prohibit us from discovering the larger freedom of the discipline we have embraced, and consequently, we will never properly play the music we study.

Likewise, some musicians become so driven and compelled that they practice continually, working themselves into a state of emotional and physical exhaustion. Furthermore, some become perfectionists, stuck on every note and passage, unable to go on to the greater perfection of the whole musical piece. Finally, some try to play it all and thus become a real master of nothing.

The same holds true with spirituality and the church. Some try to take shortcuts around the discipline of the Teacher, or hang on to personal "idiosyncrasies," and end up frustrated and failing. Others become "workaholics for Christ" and end up unable really to do His work. Others become so scrupulous over little things that they are never able to do God's greater work. Finally, some try to do so much that they end by doing nothing at all.

To do the work of Christ in the church, we must embrace a discipline under a teacher and then proceed at a moderate pace. Otherwise, we will end up frustrated and failing, no matter how well intentioned we might be.

We can all remember the overzealous religious people in

our lives. Some start out well but quickly burn out and break down. Others fall into a fanaticism in a particular prayer or Bible devotion that is ugly and lifeless. Many leave the church and the faith altogether after a few overly intense years. The last state is worse than the first. A moderate discipline avoids these traps and supports us in making beautiful music for God.

Musical Beatitudes

Finally, the good musician must discover a certain set of "beatitudes" if he really is to learn the heart and soul of the music of God.

The good musician must know his own poverty before he can receive the gift of song with a grateful and humble heart. Otherwise his heart will always be proud.

He must know how to mourn and weep from the depths of his soul, so that his song might comfort and console those who weep and mourn. Otherwise his music will remain ever aloof from the heartfelt pains, struggles, and joys common to all humankind.

He must sing his song with meekness so that a gentle strength can go forth to all the earth.

He must hunger and thirst for sacred melodies and revere them as true gifts from God. For anyone who finds melodic food and drink in the things of the world will not persevere in the divine search and will, at best, play the music of God insensitively.

He must sing a song of mercy for the weak; so he must first know his own weakness and need for mercy, his dependence on the Master.

His melody must flow forth from a humble and pure heart, for only the humble and pure of heart can hear God's song.

The words he sings must be words of peace, so that in war and persecution the weak might remain strong.

Correspondingly, in our spiritual life, the Beatitudes of Jesus Christ must form the heart of our melody and song. Without them our music remains shallow and unable to reach to the depths of the human heart and soul. Without knowing them, we will always remain on the outside of the heart of God.

This is the way of paradox. It is the way of contradiction, yet it remains the greatest truth of all the ages. This is a way that finds wealth in poverty, joy in sorrow, strength in meekness, satisfaction in the fast, the righteousness of the law in forgiving sin, purity in humble admission of one's impurity and sin, peace in the midst of war, and ultimate victory in persecution and seeming defeat. This is the way of real and eternal blessedness. This is the truth of the paradox of Jesus Christ. This is the way of the cross . . . the Paschal mystery. This is the very heart of God's melody and song. Without it the music of our life can have no lasting beauty at all.

III: The Church

*

The music born of the beatific heart is the music born of humility. Humility accepts the truth of its own gifts and is sure of the Giver. It creates a quiet confidence. But humility also accepts the truth of the gifts and talents of others. In fact, because it also accepts the truth of its own shortcomings, it is inclined to accept the gifts and talents of others before it puts forward its own. Thus, the beatific music born of a humble heart is often best played in concert with others.

The guitarist taught by the Master Musician learns that the

most beautiful music is only rarely played as a solo. It is usually played in concert with others. There are other instruments besides the guitar. Each has gone through a refining process, and each is equally precious. The Master has brought forth not only guitars and guitarists but a whole symphonic orchestra of fine instruments and quality players! He has also brought forth vocalists and a whole choir of singers who have also gone through a similar and equally profound process to develop their voices. They all await to perform the Master's song.

Humility and Love

The music of the Master is also born of love. This is the greatest music of the heart. By its very nature, love is the selfless giving of oneself for the benefit of another. Furthermore, it is the union of at least two in selfless giving to produce new life in at least a third. It is unity in trinity in even its minimal form from the beginnings of eternity. Therefore, even within the Master Himself, the music of His heart existed within the Trinity of His own being before He ever shared the gift with another living soul. In God this is seen in the union of the Father and the Son, producing the Spirit in an eternal process of begotteness and procession. In people it is mirrored in the human trinity of body, soul, and spirit. Or as the scholastics said, memory, intellect, and will. The eternal realities of the Godhead are mirrored and effected in us. In this sense both the Master and His music are eternal—the song of love existed first as communication among the Father, Son, and Spirit.

But love overflows without end, so the Master willingly shared His gift with others. Soon a symphony of players was born.

Likewise, if every player of the symphony plays the music born of love, he or she must be willing to play *with* others, *for* others. Otherwise the music is not really the music born of the

Master's love. It is born of self and will be left forever on the outside of the real music of the heart. To play the music of the heart one must play the music of humility and love, which in turn necessitates that this song be played in the humble and loving unity of the greatest symphonic orchestra.

It requires a death to the ego of self so that a greater music than any one musician, no matter how great, can perform. It requires a death to the ego of self that fulfills all who hear. It is only in this death to self that the musician can break through to the greater sense of purpose and the real fulfillment of the musical self. This is the mystery of the music born of love.

Likewise, our response of faith in Christ cannot be lived out alone. It must be lived out in community with others. It must be lived out as church. Otherwise, our faith lacks the essential ingredient of humility. It lacks the primary ingredient of love. Without humility and love, our lives can never be "like Christ" or Christian.

We recognize that we are not complete in ourselves and depend on others for our very identity. That is why we are called the body of Christ. We humbly recognize the need for others in order for ourselves to be complete. We die to ourselves for the benefit of others out of selfless love and so break through to the greatest of all self-fulfillment and life purpose. Not one of us makes up the body of Christ alone. It can only be done in union with others. Without others we cannot really be called Christian.

This confronts the rampant individualism of the West. No doubt, we have become a "me-first" society. This attitude breaks down families. It breaks down Christian communities and churches. It is even breaking down the work force. What was once heralded as the unique virtue of the West now threatens its very existence through moral and economic decline. These words sting. But we know they are true.

We seem to have forgotten that the more subtle and less

glamorous tones within the orchestra may be more important to the overall effect of the music than the "featured" instruments.

Many times we think that one instrument is more important than another, or we pick out only one or the other to listen to. This creates an imbalance in the harmony of the symphonic sound. The music was written to be heard as a whole. One instrument or section is not meant to overpower another but to blend together—to complement one another.

For the church, this means that the rich must join together with the poor; the strong with the weak. This radically challenges the materialism of the West, particularly of the United States. We are six percent of the world's population, but we consume 50-60 percent of the world's resources. Forty-two thousand people die each day from hunger-related conditions, and 40,000 of these victims are children. This is sin. It must stop, but it will only stop if we repent and commit ourselves to change.

Furthermore, those we often consider poor are rich in God's eyes. Those we consider rich are really poor. It is time for our materialistic, consumeristic, and individualistic attitudes to change. Otherwise, we cannot claim to be part of God's orchestra. We cannot really claim to know and share the Good News of Jesus Christ.

The Church and the Orchestra

The church is like an orchestra commissioned to play a beautiful symphony from God. Life in the church is never a solo performance. Oh yes, there may be various individual solos within the symphony, but the whole symphony remains a musical work of art to be performed by the orchestra as a whole. The orchestra itself is made up of individuals who are grouped together into various sections under section leaders and a conductor of the whole. Each individual is expected to have a quality instrument and to be able to play that particular instrument with near-virtuoso sensitivity and skill. The individual preparations and disciplines of a lifetime are expected of those who will be eventually chosen to be an orchestra member and play in the concert performance.

To be chosen for a real orchestra position, you must audition, or "try out" for membership. Many are called to fill the necessary membership. The orchestra is usually quite large. But from the many who respond, only a few are chosen. Usually more respond than are really needed. Only a few really have devoted the proper time to develop their craft, to attain the degree of musicianship required.

The same holds true in the church. Many are called, but only a few will actually be chosen by God to play in this divine orchestra. Only a few will be willing to endure the necessary preparations for playing God's symphony correctly.

Part of this choosing of the few happens at the end of the

world in the Judgment. Part of this choosing happens now by our life in the church and the communities and ministries of the church. Either way it is dependent on our willingness to really prepare for the greater work of God.

The divine orchestra of the church is also made up of different sections. There are string sections and woodwind sections. There are brass and percussion sections. Furthermore, some sections are broken down into smaller sections, such as first violin, second violin, viola, cello, and double bass sections—these just among the strings.

For the orchestra to sound resonant and full, these sections are also separated and carefully placed in just the right place. If they sit just anywhere, the orchestra will not sound balanced and the beautiful symphony will become a cacophony.

In the church there are not only individual gifts. There are corporate gifts. Many people may have the same gift, so they group together into movements, communities, cell, support, and prayer groups to help bring that gift to the whole church with greater clarity and strength. Thus, we not only have the individual gifts of the Spirit but the corporate gifts used in roles of service for the church and the world. Left alone, their gift remains only one weak and unclear voice in a roaring crowd. Grouped together and placed properly in the church, the voice of the gift becomes clear and strong.

The Liturgy and the Symphony

The orchestra does not play music in a haphazard way. It is given a symphony to play, with all the parts and their arrangements on sheet music.

The symphony itself is made up of thousands upon thousands of individual notes. These notes are grouped together into beautiful melodies and expansive chords. If played at the wrong time or in the wrong way, these notes become only noise.

The melodies and chords of the symphony are further grouped into various movements. Each movement of the symphony depicts a different character or mood that the composer wishes to express. Some are brash and triumphant. Others are subdued. Some are happy, while others are melancholy or sad. Trying to play all the movements at once would not communicate any mood at all, while separating them and playing them in just the right order and pace creates a greater movement that makes the whole symphony an artistic success and brings a sense of fulfillment and satisfaction to the listener.

The divine liturgy is like a symphony of God. Liturgy—formal, corporate worship—is the common prayer of the people of God. As with the symphony, the Liturgy must be assisted in, "played," by an entire company.

But liturgy is not corporate chaos. It, too, has movements that make up an experience of the whole and has individual notes that make up various melodies and chords. These notes must be played in just the right way in order for the symphony to be complete.

In a symphony there are parts to be played by everyone. Also in the liturgy and other formal expressions of worship, each individual is asked to play at different times. To be complete, the individual must participate with all his heart, mind, and skill or the whole is not really complete. Furthermore, there are little "solos" here and there where a special instrument or player is given a moment to shine. But these moments are brief. They are special and extraordinary. The full symphony never degenerates into a solo performance. *It must be played by all.*

There is also "sheet music" for this symphony. There are assigned "notes." They are actually written out on a page to make sure that everyone remembers his or her part. If the players get confused and play the wrong notes, the perfect harmony of the symphony becomes chaos and discord.

Also in the liturgy, the parts are assigned. They are

actually written out in prayers and scriptural texts. But this is not to stifle the Spirit; it helps facilitate and ensure that the harmony of the Spirit of God is heard by all.

In playing these assigned parts, something unique happens to the players, so they participate in a full expression of their own heart and soul but are making a music greater than their own individual talent. Yes, the individual musician may have played a part a little differently if left to himself. But this is willingly sacrificed for the sake of the whole. Furthermore, the good composer is able to compose in such a way as to both challenge and satisfy the individual musician of the orchestra. In some of the symphonies of the great composers, certain measures allow key soloists to improvise concerning the particulars of the part, as long as the overall direction is not jeopardized.

The same thing is true with liturgy. Each participant prays his or her assigned part. In so doing, we are transformed beyond our own limited spiritualities and prayers into the common experience of the whole church. We enter fully into this mystery. We play a symphony that is timeless and universal. It takes us beyond ourselves and into the universal experience of God through the church. Since the composer is God through the whole church, we will find ourselves both challenged and fulfilled. Furthermore, there will be some moments for personal spontaneity and the exercising of charismatic gifts written into the text.

The danger, of course, in any liturgical or formal prayer expression is the stifling of the Spirit. Many times the formal and liturgical prayers subtly come to substitute for a more personal faith experience so that in the end, little personal faith remains at all. But if a living, personal faith is retained, the "symphony" of the liturgy can be an awesome and faith-filled experience indeed.

The Sacraments

The symphony is not only liturgical. It is sacramental. It is mysterious. It communicates the love of God that is beyond all knowledge. In a very real way, music represents and symbolizes the heart and soul of the composer. But it doesn't just represent and symbolize. In a way beyond words, the heart and soul of the composer are actually present in spirit when the music is reverently performed. He comes to us under the form of the music. Through the human mediation of the players, the interpretation of the conductor, and even the notes on the page, the spirit communicates to us.

The same thing is true with the sacraments. The "notes on the page" are like the word of God in the prayers he has commended and Scripture. These words are powerful in and of themselves. They are like dynamite waiting to be ignited. They break through to eternity. The power of God resides in this divine word, just waiting to be spoken.

The players are like the various liturgical participants, and the conductor is like the presiding minister. Yet, through all of these instruments the "music" of God is still played. The heart and soul of the Composer is really present. God is the Composer; the music, His sacraments.

The Conductor

Of course, the whole orchestra must come under the leadership of a conductor if it is to play a symphony. Even the best of orchestras finds it almost impossible to play even the most perfectly composed symphony when there is no conductor. Even though there is clearly marked sheet music, the notes, melodies, and movements can and must be rightly interpreted by the conductor in order for the symphony to sound pleasing to the listener. In fact, a conductor can and usually does greatly enhance or detract from the composition by his own interpretation of the musical score.

The same thing holds true in the church. On one level Jesus Himself is our conductor. But on another level the church needs a visible conductor, or leader, to keep her from breaking into disharmony and even chaos. As with an orchestra, there can only be one conductor at a time. We have been given a "score," or sheet music, in the Scriptures, our sacred traditions, and our ecumenical councils. But even these must be authoritatively interpreted and implemented. This is why Jesus left the church under the leadership of the apostles, who were themselves led by Simon Peter. It was all part of Jesus' chosen plan. His choices established an enduring pattern.

This is also true with our formal patterns of worship. Even though various denominations have established clear directions through laws, customs, and other means, this "score" must be interpreted by a "conductor" of each "orchestra." This happens in each local church, parish, and diocese, and in the church universal. This is done through the ministry of local pastors and bishops, and through the councils and conventions of Protestant, Catholic, and Orthodox churches. In the Catholic church of which I am a member, this is done based on scriptural, historical precedent most perfectly through the bishop of Rome and the Ecumenical Council. This leadership is essential lest our symphony break down and fragment permanently into smaller ensembles, folk groups, and street bands. They might also be good, as we shall see, but they can never match the full grandeur and majesty of a full symphony. Of course, the liturgy itself is an earthly symbol of the entire church life and prefigures heavenly realities.

The conductors of the symphony must be extraordinary and balanced individuals. While they themselves are usually quite capable musicians, much more than being a virtuoso of only one particular instrument is required of the conductors of a full orchestra. The "score" must be second nature to them. They must also understand the orchestra. They must know the history of each instrument and its present capabilities. They must also know players' abilities and needs and, to some extent, their real-life situation. Otherwise they will never be able to bring the very best music out of them, either as individuals or as a whole.

This is also true in the church. The "conductors," or presiders, on any level, must be able to see and grasp all that they are leading. While not necessarily "expert" in all at their command, they must at least have a general working knowledge of all under their command.

They must also have living knowledge of the Composer. They must know God through a personal love relationship with Jesus. The "score," or the Scripture, sacred tradition, and liturgical canons, must come to their minds as naturally as breathing. They must also understand their "orchestra," or the people of God, as church. They must know their needs and abilities. they must know them as a corporate whole and as individuals. Only then will the presiding minister bring the best "performance" out of his orchestra.

There are, of course, other roles of leadership in the symphony orchestra. There is the "concert master," usually the first violinist, who stands next in command to the conductor. He represents the players to the conductor and vice versa. There are also leaders of each instrumental section, such as first viola, first cello, and so on. They see to it that their particular section is properly in order and ready to perform. Then there are also the more administrative roles of leadership that are never even visible in the orchestral performances. Invariably there are sometimes tensions between those who play the performing roles and those who take the administrative ones.

The same is true in the church. We have our "section leaders" and "concert masters" in auxiliary bishops, associate pastors, and vicar ministers, or in choir leaders, lectors, servers, and ushers, for example. We also have apostles, prophets, teachers (both clerics and lay), who lead the various "sections" of this ecclesial symphony orchestra in cell and support groups or base Christian communities. We also must have some administrative leaders. God knows we have a multitude of "boards" that often think they can play everything! Needless to say, there is often tension between the more "hands-on" ministries and the administrators. But really, both are necessary in the well-run church.

Other Forms: The Chamber Orchestra and Concertos

As we have alluded to above, there are also other forms of musical companies. The full orchestra and symphony might be the most expensive and grand combination, but it is not the only one. If our music of God is to really be abundant and full, we must also appreciate the other combinations as well.

As well as the full symphony, there are "concertos." These

are usually designed to highlight the beauty of a particular instrument and its solo capabilities. Consequently, the soloist plays much of the work himself, taking most of the melodies while being accompanied by the orchestra. There will probably be prolonged passages in which the soloist plays totally alone without the accompaniment of the orchestra at all.

Depending on the character of the featured instrument of the concerto, the orchestra itself may be reduced in size so as not to overpower the soloist. This downsized group is often called a "chamber" orchestra.

Most of the same roles of the full orchestra and symphony apply to the concerto and chamber orchestra, but they are played in a different setting. There remain sections in the orchestra, the sheet music or score, and a conductor. The main differences are the highlighted soloist and the reduced size of the orchestra. Although not quite as universal and complete, the concerto is more personal and intimate.

The same thing is true in the church. There are times for "concertos" rather than "symphonies." A particular gift of an individual minister or layperson needs the time and place to shine. Furthermore, the smaller configurations of the orchestra allow for greater intimacy and personal ministry. These ministries and gatherings still operate under certain directives and norms, or "sheet music," and must still be "conducted" by the pastoral guidance of the appropriate leader of the church, but the nature of the event remains somewhat different from the gathering of the full orchestra to play the complete symphony.

These "concertos" are represented by the various movements and communities in the church. All through the ages, founders and foundresses have been raised up by the Spirit to live certain aspects of the gospel more radically. This is seen especially in the monastic and religious tradition as well as in some of the more intense expressions of Protestant churches. In the paraliturgical gatherings of the church, individual lay and clerical leaders' individual gifts are allowed to "shine" especially, too.

The Ensemble

The chamber ensemble consists of an even smaller group of instruments than the concerto, with a repertoire written just for these instruments. This can be heard in groups like string quartets, horn, or even guitar ensembles. Usually the music is still very technically precise and requires an almost virtuoso skill. It is usually, at least initially, read off sheet music. Furthermore, the ensemble usually has a leader. But unlike the more formal "conductor," the leader, or "director" sits among the players as one of the more talented members.

We also have such "ensembles" in the church. They are our "cell groups" of twelve or so members. They range from charismatic to spontaneous to highly structured. Let us begin with those who choose to follow a more structured and technically precise "song" for their particular gathering. There is not usually much "improvisation" in these kinds of groups. They have a spiritual method, or outline, and they choose to stay pretty much "to the book." They are usually not very much into spontaneous or charismatic expressions of prayer or ministry. This is seen in some of the older third orders and guilds, or the newer expressions such as Marriage Encounter or Cursillio in the Catholic Church. It is perhaps best represented by non-pentecostal renewal-oriented groups within the Baptist, Methodist, or Presbyterian churches in the Protestant circles. *This way is safe. It is tested and sure.*

They, too, have a leader who does not stand formally before them but sits among them as a fellow "player." Usually, the leader's position has come to him by nature of his skill at performing the "music" they have all gathered to play.

It must be admitted that the appeal of ensemble music is limited. It lacks the expansiveness of the full orchestra and symphony, the personal intimacy of the chamber orchestra, and the spontaneity of other groups, but it remains a viable and legitimate expression for some. Likewise, in the church the more structured and safe cell group is not as popular as today's more personal, spontaneous, and pentecostal support group. But there are still many who find that cell groups enhance their life of faith within the larger church. Many more may yet find this expression safer as the cell group phenomenon spreads throughout our mainstream churches.

The Concert Hall, the Ballroom, and the Club

It would be good to mention here that the various forms of music and groupings of musicians can be played in different settings. The symphony, the concerto, the ensemble, and most concerts of other less formal forms of music can rightly be played in the concert hall. Some, though, are best played in smaller recital halls or studios. Formal dance music is usually played in the ballroom. The least formal of musical styles is best performed in dance halls or clubs to allow a more free and informal response from the audience.

The same is true in the church. Some gatherings are best facilitated in majestic cathedrals, sanctuaries, or large parish churches. Other gatherings are best suited for large halls less used for liturgical worship. Others take place in small chapels or social halls. Still others might be best taken care of outside in a setting similar to Christ's own Sermon on the Mount. Often, those who like one particular setting become critical of other settings or the people who prefer one different from theirs. This is not right. We should all learn to appreciate the uniquely good qualities of all settings. While it is normal to have your own personal preferences, others may prefer different settings.

Mutual tolerance and appreciation serve to enrich the whole church rather than to split her into factions, each meeting only in its own favorite space. There should be some healthy tolerance and interaction.

The Jazz and Pop Groups

The jazz and pop ensemble is perhaps one of the most dazzling and brilliant of all corporate musical possibilities. But it can also be one of the most dangerous. The jazz group is made up of highly skilled musicians able to play both the most difficult of the classics and the most spontaneous and adventurous modern and popular compositions. It can also reintegrate the beauties of the ancient and primitive forms of music with the developments of the modern era. The music is itself highly intricate and rivals the genius of classical music when seen on sheet music. However, it also leaves room for much personal interpretation and improvisation by both the individual players and the group as a whole. Jazz, which can easily be one of the most expressive and adventurous of all musical forms, can also lead to the danger of producing musical show-offs who are musical "fast guns," or who play music only for music's sake. Ironically, the form that perhaps best accommodates the real expression of the human soul through music can easily degenerate into a music turned in on itself, producing only musical egoists and music for music's sake.

The same thing is true in the church. Our charismatic and spontaneous prayer groups are like our "jazz groups." They can rival the spiritual classics in many of their insights and experiences, but they can also lead to real spiritual egoism and pride. In themselves these "jazz groups" of the church are perhaps the best suited to fully integrate all the spiritual gifts from God. Ironically, though, they often produce a spiritual music that is more caught up in the show of the gifts than in the real worship of the giver.

The Folk Group

The folk ensemble is quite literally a "group of folks" who play the music of the people. They play the simple songs that touch and express a people's heart. The music might be simple and childlike indeed, but it can be quite profound in its simplicity. Indeed, the folk songs of a people have often provided the elegantly simple melodies of some of the great symphonies. The group usually has a "leader" among the performers, and while certain chords and melodies and lyrics are followed, a certain amount of simple improvisation is possible. The danger of folk music is that it can sometimes put excessive limitations on the more majestic and expansive musical tendencies of a composer, a performer, and a people, if left entirely to itself.

Likewise, in the church we, too, have our "folk groups" that demonstrate a popular piety and lifestyle that is both simple and profound in its childlike humility. Sometimes this piety becomes the basis for great spiritual achievements and the attainment of great mystical heights. Left only to itself, however, this childlike piety can actually work to prohibit the more majestic and awesome aspects of God from being recognized or expressed.

Worse yet, the spiritual folk group can sometimes degenerate from childlike humility into only *childishness*. Here real simplicity degenerates into an approach that is only simplistic. It prohibits real wealth in the Spirit. It inhibits real spiritual growth. These groups usually have a leader in their midst. While they follow a certain "form" in their gatherings and structures, there is still room for some simple and limited "improvisation" or spontaneous expressions. The folk group of the church remains an essential link with the real spiritual songs of the average people of a given culture.

The Rock Band

One of the folk expressions of modern culture is rock 'n' roll. Even the controversial rock band has lessons to teach us. These lessons are both negative and positive.

It has been said that, born in a rebellious time in a rebellious nation, rock music has little positive to offer. rock 'n' roll has been called an adolescent music for an adolescent culture. That culture has become America and the Western world.

No doubt, some of these observations are true. Even its name, "rock 'n' roll," originates from African-American slang for illicit and adolescent-like sexual behavior.

Its music tends to push both voices and instruments to a

strained and unnatural limit. The rock voice is both underdeveloped and unnatural, constricting the throat muscles and pushing and straining for volume all at once. It is like driving a car with the brake on. The rock "tones" themselves are often "distortions" of pure tones as seen in the distorted sounds of guitar, voices, and synthesizers. Its "synthesis" comes from distortion of the pure rather than from the integrated union of pure tones to produce a stronger sound as a whole without losing the integrity of either particular tone. Therefore, these and similar observations by others have won for rock 'n' roll the seeming and often deserved reputation among the sophisticated of being a perverse and demented musical style.

On the positive side, rock can express much of the "pathos" of the human struggles. Its vocal tones express the cries of a people caught in the evils of slavery. Its "base nature" also enables it to integrate and express the ancient and primitive modes and tones spoken of above. How like the noise of the modern city is this music! The freeways, the subway train, the airports, and fire-breathing factories are all expressed in its disturbing rage.

Furthermore, the loud volume and distortions of pure sound express that which defies the natural tones and sounds of this earth. The "synthesis" of such sounds expresses the new creation that comes from the death of the old. When this synthesis is used as a sound unto itself and not as a cheap imitation or perversion of another pure acoustic sound, it is, no doubt, legitimate. Rock is "power music" and can express the powers beyond this world in both their positive and negative realities.

There is also "rock 'n' roll" in the church. In the negative, Satan and his demons are only distortions and perversions of the purity of God and His Creation. They have no power to create. They can only pervert. This is, after all, the essence of all evil, sin, and heresy. The concept of "synthesis," so popular in many spiritualities and theologies today, often has its roots in the perversion of pure spirit and thought, in order to bring only the appearance of the old or the new. Furthermore, some movements and communities get stuck in the power and aggressiveness of perpetual adolescence that fails to lead on to maturity.

On the positive side, sometimes the rebellious independence of adolescence is a necessary transitional stage from childish dependency to the mature interdependence of adulthood. Sometimes it is necessary to push away forcefully in order to embrace in union with another by mutual choice. Rock's primitive nature puts us in tune with the ancient and primitive expressions of all religion, not to mention Christianity itself and its various street-level renewal movements.

Moreover, the sheer Spirit power of spiritual "rock 'n' roll" seems to distort all of our natural capacities to assimilate sound in hearing. It seems to be distortion, but it is not the sound that is distorted, only the natural reception of the "ear." Sometimes the problem is not in the music but in our capacity to hear so much volume at once.

Furthermore, sometimes we need good to use the things of a culture in order to evangelize a culture. Sometimes we must use marginal means to bring those stuck in the margin back into the mainstream or moderate middle. If a culture is stuck in the adolescent stage of spiritual "rock 'n' roll," then sometimes we must use that same "rock 'n' roll" to reach the culture in order to take it on to maturity. After all, isn't this what Jesus Himself did when He took on our humanity to lead us to divinity in Him?

We do well, then, to allow a little spiritual rock 'n' roll in the church. It keeps us young. It keeps us alive. It keeps us evangelistic and prophetic. Otherwise, we might find that in excluding a whole generation of people and believers, we are excluding Jesus Himself.

The Soloist

There are also times when we enter the concert hall or club not to hear the orchestra, chamber ensemble, band, or group but to hear a soloist. There are already solos in the symphony or concerto, the ensemble piece or song, but there still remains a deeper need in both the performer and the audience for a more personal and intimate performance. This can only be done in the complete solo performance. Here the strength and power of the group is temporarily set aside to discover the more subtle and personal touches of the soloist. Here, there is no need for a leader or conductor. The soloist simply interprets and plays by his or her own authority from the heart, interpreting the notes on the page quite personally, or choosing to improvise—the most free musical expression of the individual human heart. Nothing is quite so naked as the soloist who stands totally exposed concerning both personal talent and personal emotion. It can be incredibly disastrous, or incredibly glorious.

Because of the advanced "cutting edge" nature of the solo, beginners should wait before attempting such a performance. Take time in the orchestra to learn from the expertise of those around you. Furthermore, the soloist never gets this privilege by his or her own self will. The conductor makes these assignments. They must be earned.

There are also times for soloists in the church. There are times for individual ministers to stand before the people in their individual ministries. This can be done one-on-one in private, before a small cell group, or before a large congregation. In any case, the minister stands spiritually naked before those to whom he or she ministers. It is the minister quite personally and intimately sharing his or her understanding and experiences of the love and truth of God. The minister cannot rely on others at this point. Oh yes, there may still be a liturgical or scriptural text. But it remains for the Spirit incarnationally and personally working in and through the personal minister as well as the text to bring the full ministry of the living God to the people. The minister is free to interpret and improvise to a certain point— he or she may even improvise entirely on certain occasions— both the minister and the people need this expression. Understand how frightening such exposure can be. Nevertheless, it is also glorious to stand alone in the Spirit of our personal God, who ministers in personal ways to his people. Nothing can replace this experience.

The solo is also played in prayer. There are times for community, but there are also times for solitude. There is an irreplaceable gift received in corporate prayer with others, but the gift of solitude is also irreplaceable. As in solo ministry, solitary prayer is a naked exposure before God. It can be frightening, but it can also be glorious. It can be the most personal of all our prayer encounters with God.

This has been lived out most vividly by the Christian hermits and communities or colonies of hermits that make a special place in their lives for this solitary dimension of prayer. It is also, to a greater or lesser degree, a valid and necessary part of every Christian's life.

But we must be careful that such "solos" in ministry or lifestyle are not just mere escapes from people or from God, Himself. This is why such "solos" of solitary ministry and prayer are best discerned in union with the "conductor" of our church or community. Evangelists, teachers, and prophets are never to embark on a ministry on their own initiative. They must be sent by God and the church community.

Let those who are afraid of the group beware of the solo, and let those who are afraid of the solo beware of the group. Let those who are afraid of community beware of solitude and those who are afraid of solitude beware of community. If our solo is simply an escape from the mutual responsibility for excellence that goes with the group, then our solo is selfish. It cannot be an expression of love. If our participation in the group is merely an escape from the personal responsibility of standing naked so as to expose our real talent and emotion, then it, too, is illegitimate and dishonest.

Likewise in the church: Let those who are afraid of ministering under authority or as a team beware of ministering alone in stark, naked honesty and exposure, and let those afraid of ministering alone beware of hiding behind the security of the group. In prayer, let those who are afraid of the corporate and communal structures of liturgy, sacrament, and hierarchy in prayer beware of the so-called freedom of solitude; and let those who are afraid of the stark, naked honesty of a personal love relationship with Jesus beware of the more impersonal corporate security of liturgy, sacrament, and hierarchy.

What about our tendency to just "run away" from others when life with others gets too tough? Be it marriages, jobs, churches, or religious vocations, most of the "rugged individual-ists" of Western society cannot face the truly rugged aspect of tough love when it is meted out to them in community. It is always easier to "run away." But it is never easy to play a legitimate "solo" in the midst of God's symphony orchestra. It takes incredible training, fortitude, and courage. How well we remember those who have run away. How little we really appreciate those who have stayed.

The Future and New Integrations

As we look to the future, we see that each of these expressions of the church has something good to offer. They also have their own unique dangers. No one expression has it all. By creatively integrating them together, the good of each is preserved and enhanced, while the dangers are offset, checked, and balanced.

In music I have found that some of the most creative and new compositions integrate several or all of these styles of the past as they try to discover something new. If you listen, you can clearly pick out the various influences. The integrity of each has been retained. but they have joined together to create something that moves into the future.

This is not synthesis. Synthesis usually perverts, bends, and distorts a pure sound to create the illusion of another, either old or new. *Integration* unites pure sound and tone to form a whole, bigger than any one particular part, without destroying the integrity or credibility of any of the parts. Like several cords woven into a strong rope, it creates something new from the union of the old without destroying either the old or the new.

The same is true in musical performance. I thoroughly enjoy the accurate performance of a historical piece of music from the past on the authentic instruments of the period. But I enjoy even more the combination of various historic groups to create a new performance of new music for our own era and age, one that is both ancient and modern, traditional and contemporary. Any of the smaller groups and soloists can be successfully combined with the symphony orchestra to create a sound and performance that is thoroughly thrilling.

The rock band, the folk group, or the jazz ensemble can all join effectively with the symphony orchestra; the symphony is best equipped to integrate them all.

Similarly, various smaller groups and soloists can come together in various combinations filled with both creative tension and harmonic peace. Furthermore, brand new combinations of orchestra, ensemble, group, band, or soloist, still await the creative composers and artists of our time and the future.

Such combinations are also true regarding the setting for such a performance. Sometimes you can use a concert hall or outdoor pavilion. At other times you can use a club or an outdoor park. This all depends on the size and purpose of the gathering.

All of this is also true in the development of the church. The full-blown liturgical and sacramental celebrations of the "symphony" can easily become the integrative host of all other expressions. It is this "symphony" that can perhaps best integrate every other group, but this means that there has to be real mutual respect and humility and a real attitude of give-and-take. The "orchestra" must make free room for and fully support the other less formal and structured expressions, while the other expressions must fully acknowledge and humbly respect the full weight, power, and mystical authority in the "symphony orchestra" of the full liturgical and sacramental expression of the church. This can be difficult to maintain, but the results are genuinely awe-inspiring and well worth the challenge. I might add that similar integrations are possible between all the various expressions of the church and can be achieved with really gratifying results if undertaken in a spirit of mutual love, respect, and service to God and people.

At other times we must leave each expression free to be what it truly is without always forcing it into the inherent tension of such integrations. There are times, for instance, when I just want to hear classical music for what it is. The same holds true for ancient, sacred, folk, jazz, or rock.

This is also true in the church. There are times to just let the good of the Protestant be appropriately Protestant, or the good of the traditional Catholic be appropriately Catholic . . . only now with the added recognition of the substantial goodness and validity of one another's essential and spiritual approach to God. This is also true not only of various denominational groups but of spiritual movements and styles—charismatic or contemplative, the liturgical and spontaneous, the cell group and the larger parish. All can be integrated, but each must also have the "space" to be uniquely what they are without the constant challenge and tension of forced integration into the greater whole.

Of course, this means that we are all called to a new dynamic integration without destroying the integrity of the old. We are called to build squarely on the living stones of tradition that have come before, leaning neither to the right or to the left lest the wall we are building begins to lean and collapse. Yet we are called to go *into higher space* where no tradition has ever gone before. Otherwise, we no longer build. We simply stand still. We are called to be living stones in the building of the temple of the Spirit of God.

We can see this integration already at work in the church. Catholics and Protestants are already joining together to help evangelize the world and to bring relief and development to the poor. Their respective theologians are already meeting to break down age-old barriers of archaic and outdated thought.

Perhaps the most obvious are the Protestant clergy and

parishes that are coming into full union with Rome. While retaining that which is uniquely good and proper in their own expression, they present an exciting pattern and model. These clergy and parishes address anew the possibilities in our rich and ancient Christian heritage, from the options of a married and celibate priesthood to various liturgical forms of leadership and of worship. These clergy and their parishes come from the Eastern churches, the Protestant churches, other even more conservative, ancient traditions of the church—like the Copts—and the modern base and integrated monastic communities. Their integrated presence opens the way to the further development of the more limited and modern expressions of the West. It calls us to rediscover the charismatic balance of flexibility and discipline as seen in the various monastic and lay community movements of Christian history.

Also worth reconsideration are the more flexible and biblical structures of the apostolic and patristic eras, such as the balance between the apostles, their successors, and the prophets in their roles as clerical and lay leaders, both administrative and liturgical. Of course, all this is done by Catholics in union with the bishops and the pope and by Protestants in union with their respective leadership. It is done by a mutual respect of legitimate gifts and leadership in all, by all. It paves the way for a reuniting of the church that recognizes the legitimate diversity of each expression. It paves the way toward the future.

A new integrated unity is possible on every level of the church, just as it is with the symphony orchestra and other expressions, if we will just take the risk both to work for it and let it happen. On one level it is the most natural thing in the world. On another level it is supernatural and divine. On every level the results can be astonishingly gratifying.

We must also not be afraid to reach back to the ancient music of pre-Christian times. These traditions all have defects, to be sure, but they all have something good to offer as well that recognizes the goodness of God in all peoples and cultures of the world.

In like manner, in the church we must not be afraid to integrate the good from other ancient peoples and world religions into the one sheepfold of Christ. Yes, they all have defects. The fullness of truth and love is found only in Christ. But truth and goodness are gifts from God. All people of good will, all philosophy, all religions are given by God to lead all to Christ. Only when they become obstacles to that journey towards their fulfillment in Christ do they become evil.

Conclusion

*

So the symphony is now ready to play. The conductor stands poised with baton in hand. The score lies open, with the notes just waiting to be interpreted and played. Each finely crafted instrument is polished and shined to accentuate the fine proportions and quality craftsmanship given it from its creator. Each player sits poised in exactly the proper position to get the maximum performance from his or her instrument. Behind each note played will be years and years of disciplined and heartfelt preparation and training. All seems ready now. Both the orchestra and the audience wait with eager anticipation for the music to begin.

We do well to remember that the music of the symphony at any time or place on earth can only partially reflect and embody the full music of the Master Musician's eternal and infinite heart. He is at once both fully present within and beyond any enclosure or limitation. This is the ultimate paradox and mystery. Like a sacrament or religious icon of the church, where the real presence of God can be full but not enclosed, the music can symbolize and embody in this life the deeper eternal and infinite music of the heart. Yet this music defies all human limitations, categories, or sounds.

As the Godhead fully resided in Jesus yet was not enclosed, and Jesus resides within the sacrament without being enclosed, so the fullness of the Master Musician's heart resides in his music yet is never enclosed. Perhaps the full music of eternity can best be heard only in silence.

In this sense, the symphony is only a doorway to the real music of the soul. The Master Musician has used the instruments, the musicians, and the symphonic orchestra of Creation to usher us into the concert hall of eternity. He has used the finite to usher us into the infinite, the things of time to usher us to the eternal, and the human to usher us to the divine. He took on humanity to lead us all to divinity. He took on the things of death and death itself to lead us to eternal life. In this sense, the things of this world are indispensable. They are necessary and good. They are His gifts of grace to all who yearn to hear the Master's song.

But the earthly symphony is not the absolute fullness of His heavenly song. It never will be, as long as it sojourns on the face of this earth. It embodies one but it also prefigures its full heavenly reality. This can only be heard in the hidden recesses of the heart. It might affect it. It might stir it. But it can never fully replicate it. That is reserved for eternity alone. For now we know God in the faintly familiar melodies of the human soul. Or perhaps would know absolutely in silence.

So let us listen to the symphony. Let us join in. Let it stir the heart. Let it affect the soul. Let us find the real presence of the Master Musician's soul within it. But let us also remember that it is only a reflection of the Master Musician's melody and song. He is as fully present as is possible in this life. It is only a doorway for the divine. Let us never make of this symphony a god. It ever remains but a gift from the one true God. It remains a gift of the Master Musician.

The Rehearsal and the Concert

In the final analysis, we must recognize that anything we do or develop in this life is only in rehearsal for the concert and performance of eternity. The "concert" comes in the next life. This is only "rehearsal." The final performance is still ahead. We are in the "kindergarten" of the school of eternity.

This means that while we must strive for excellence and development, there is still room for trial and error. There will be some inevitable mistakes made. There will be sins. We are all only human. We must be willing to forgive ourselves and others our mistakes so that we can keep working through this dress rehearsal of the eternal concert.

If we do not forgive mistakes, then there can be no eventual concert. Furthermore, if we do not keep trying to get better, there can be no concert performance at all. Even in the dress rehearsal there are chances to correct and forgive last-minute mistakes and changes.

In the Christian recording industry, there is a saying, "Life is a take." In other words, life is serious. We are being recorded . . . recorded by God! Every thought, word, and action is known to God and actually recorded by God. This means that we should not take life lightly or piddle away valuable time with thoughtless scales played while just "warming up." The time is short. The record light is on!

There can, however, be more than one "take" in a recording session. In the end, you can use the best one, or even edit together the best part of each to produce an excellent whole. This means that much of the weaker parts of even the recorded "takes" are never used. They are, in a sense, still rehearsals for the recorded concert performance.

The record light causes the inexperienced musician to tense up and actually make more mistakes than usual. For the experienced professional, the record light simply causes him or her to play a little more seriously that which is almost second nature already. If the professional makes some mistakes, then he knows that another take and/or edit of more than one take will be tried.

This easygoing seriousness is the best attitude used in recording sessions. It is also the best attitude used in life. It can only be reached through experience. There are no shortcuts to the attitude of an experienced musician. Likewise, there are no shortcuts to spiritual maturity in Christ. It only comes through living experience.

Praise God that we are given rehearsal time on earth before the concert of eternity! The record light might be on, but we are given more than one take. Life is serious, but it is not unforgivable. Given this balance, Jesus frees us to become the best spiritual musicians. He has made of our life an instrument to make music for God. Now it is up to us to respond. Now we must become experienced and balanced musicians. Together, we must become a fully integrated symphony orchestra to make music that the world has never heard before.

Will you make this music? Or will your life be incomplete, or even silent? Will you join the orchestra, or will you remain in a smaller group, your music incomplete? Dare to respond. Take the risk. Begin the spiritual work of a musician for God.

Let Him first craft us into a fine musical instrument. Then let us learn to play under his expert instructions. Then, let us join in the symphony orchestra of the church and make a beautiful music bigger than any one musician for all the people of the world.